Wolfgang Amadeus Mozart

PIANO CONCERTOS
Nos. 11–16

In Full Score

With Mozart's Cadenzas for Nos. 12–16

From the Breitkopf & Härtel
Complete Works Edition

Dover Publications, Inc.
New York

Published in Canada by General Publishing Company, Ltd.,
30 Lesmill Road, Don Mills, Toronto, Ontario.
Published in the United Kingdom by Constable and Company, Ltd.

This Dover edition, first published in 1987, is a republication of
portions of *Serie 16 (Concerte für das Pianoforte)* of *Wolfgang Amadeus
Mozart's Werke. Kritisch durchgesehene Gesammtausgabe*, originally
published by Breitkopf & Härtel, Leipzig, 1877–1879. The specific
portions included here, comprising the complete Piano Concertos
Nos. 11–16, appeared in 1878. To these have been added the cadenzas for Nos. 12–16, extracted from *Serie 22 (Kleinere Stücke für das
Pianoforte)* of the same general work, as published in 1878.

The publisher is grateful to the Paul Klapper Library of Queens
College for making its copy of the cadenzas available for reproduc-
tion.

Manufactured in the United States of America
Dover Publications, Inc., 31 East 2nd Street, Mineola, N.Y. 11501

Library of Congress Cataloging-in-Publication Data

Mozart, Wolfgang Amadeus, 1756–1791.
 [Concertos, piano, orchestra. Selections]
 Piano concertos nos. 11–16.

 Reprint. Previously published: Leipzig : Breitkopf & Härtel, 1878.
 Originally published in series: Wolfgang Amadeus Mozart's
Werke. Kritisch durchgesehene. Serie 16, 22.
 Contents: No. 11 in F major, K. 413 (1782–83)—No. 12 in A major,
K. 414 (1782)—[etc.]—No. 16 in D major, K. 451 (1784)
 1. Concertos (Piano)—Scores.
M1010.M95B59   1987   87-750987
ISBN 0-486-25468-2

Contents

Note: The concerto numbers given here, those of the *Gesammtausgabe*, are still in general use. Cuthbert Girdlestone, however, in his important study *Mozart and His Piano Concertos*, does not recognize four early works as true concertos and numbers the six pieces included here as Nos. 7–12, respectively. All the cadenzas collectively have the Köchel number 624. Not included here are two cadenzas for No. 11, in Leopold Mozart's handwriting, not published until 1921 and generally considered authentic.

Note: The W.A.M. numbers at the foot of each page are the same as the Köchel numbers for the respective compositions.

Piano Concerto No. 11 in F Major, K.413

4

Adagio.   in tempo

W. A. M. 413.

SOLO

TUTTI

W. A. M. 413.

W. A. M. 413.

W.A.M. 413.

19

W. A. M. 413.

W.A.M. 413.

W.A.M.413.

W. A. M. 413.

TUTTI

SOLO

W. A. M. 413.

W.A.M. 413.

Piano Concerto No. 12 in A Major, K.414

SOLO.

W. A.M. 414.

Sec. 3

Sec. 4

legato

legato

TUTTI.

SOLO.

R-ST

legato

Codetta (from ST)

TUTTI.

W. A. M. 414.

CODA (T)

W. A. M. 414.

SOLO.

TUTTI.

SOLO.

W.A.M. 414.

W. A. M. 414.

W. A. M. 414.

TUTTI.

W. A. M. 414.

Piano Concerto No. 13 in C Major, K.415

W. A. M. 415.

TUTTI

Codetta 1

Codetta 2 (Tr. 1)

TUTTI

Andante.

Oboi.

Fagotti.

Corni in F.

Pianoforte.

Violino I.

Violino II.

Viola.

Violoncello e
Basso.

SOLO

legato

W. A. M. 415.

W. A. M. 415.

W. A. M. 415.

W. A. M. 415.

SOLO

Adagio.

Piano Concerto No. 14 in E-flat Major, K.449

W. A. M. 449.

W. A. M. 449.

114

W. A. M. 449.

Andantino.
TUTTI.

Andantino.

TUTTI.   SOLO.

Allegro ma non troppo.

Allegro ma non troppo.

W. A. M. 449.

W. A. M. 449.

W. A. M. 449.

W. A. M. **449**.

Piano Concerto No. 15 in B-flat Major, K.450

30

40

W.A.M. 450.

136

143

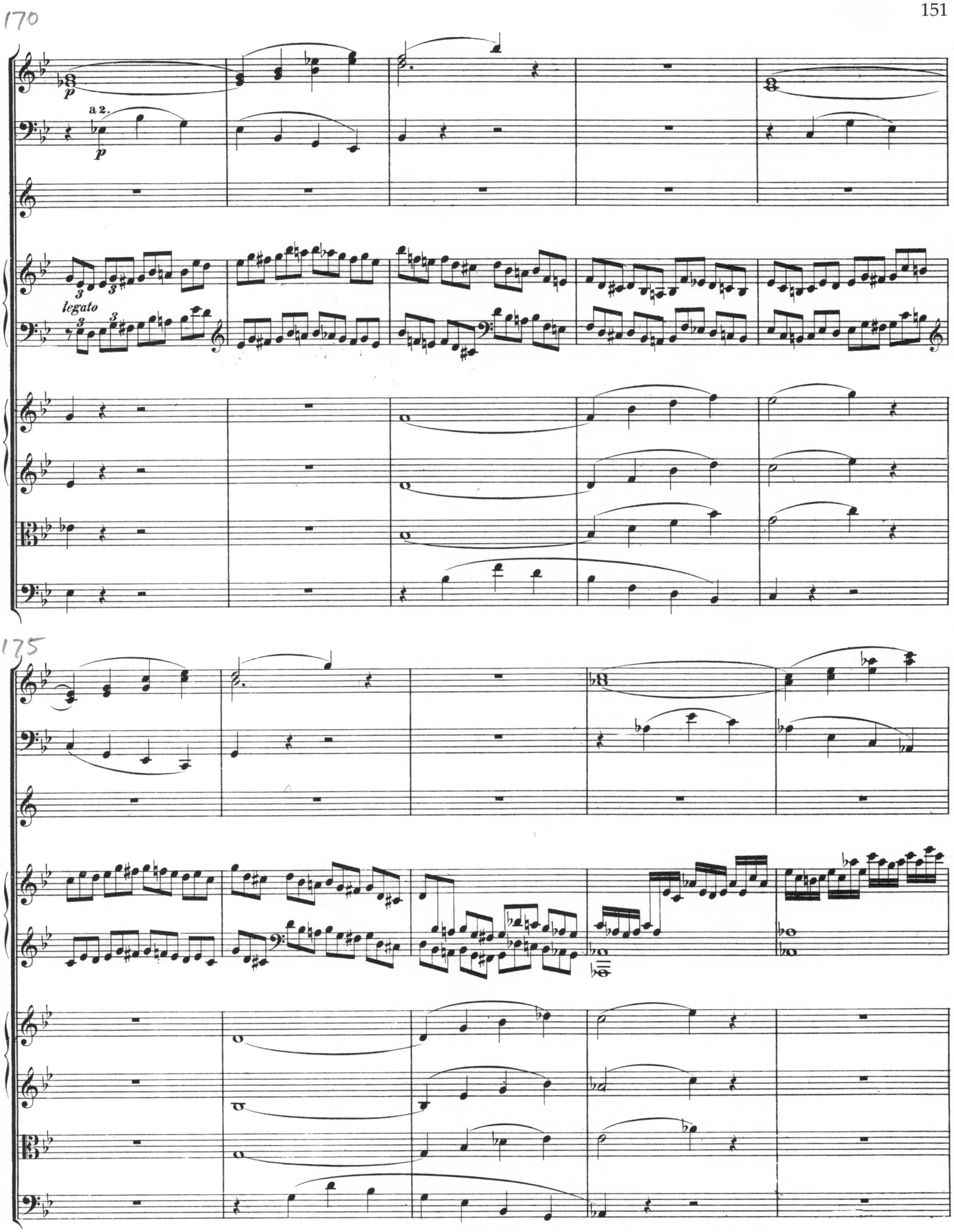
170
a 2.
p
p
legato
175

200

207

TUTTI

SOLO

TUTTI

W.A.M.450.

SOLO

W.A.M.450.

SOLO

W.A.M. 450.

TUTTI

SOLO

TUTTI

SOLO

Cadenza

183

W.A.M.450.

W.A.M.450.

Piano Concerto No. 16 in D Major, K.451

W. A. M. 451.

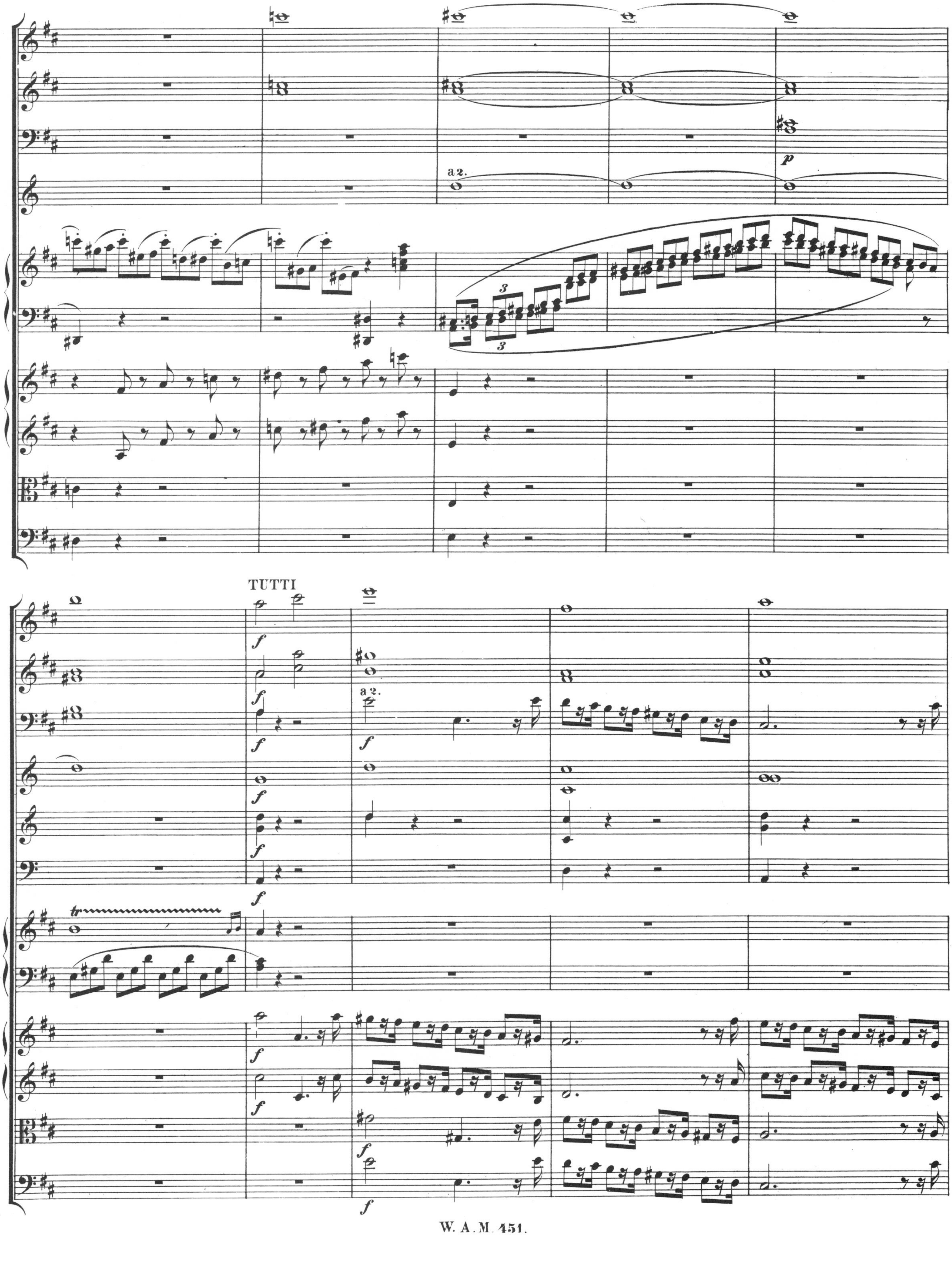
a2.
p
TUTTI
f
a2.
tr

TUTTI

I.

SOLO

W. A. M. 451.

W.A.M.451.

TUTTI

SOLO

TUTTI

SOLO

228

TUTTI

W. A M. 451.

TUTTI

SOLO

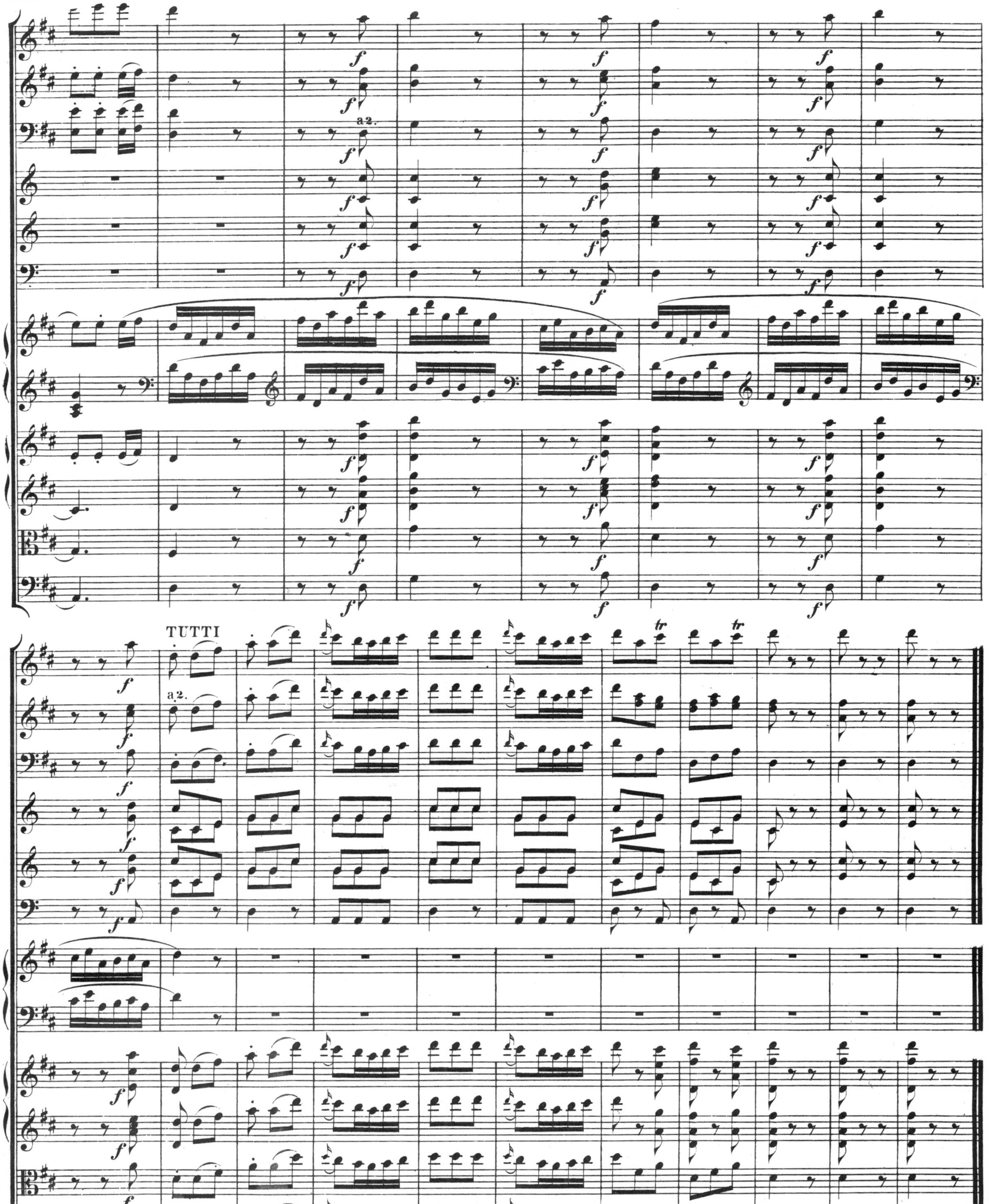
a2.
f
TUTTI
tr

Concerto No. 12, 1st Movement

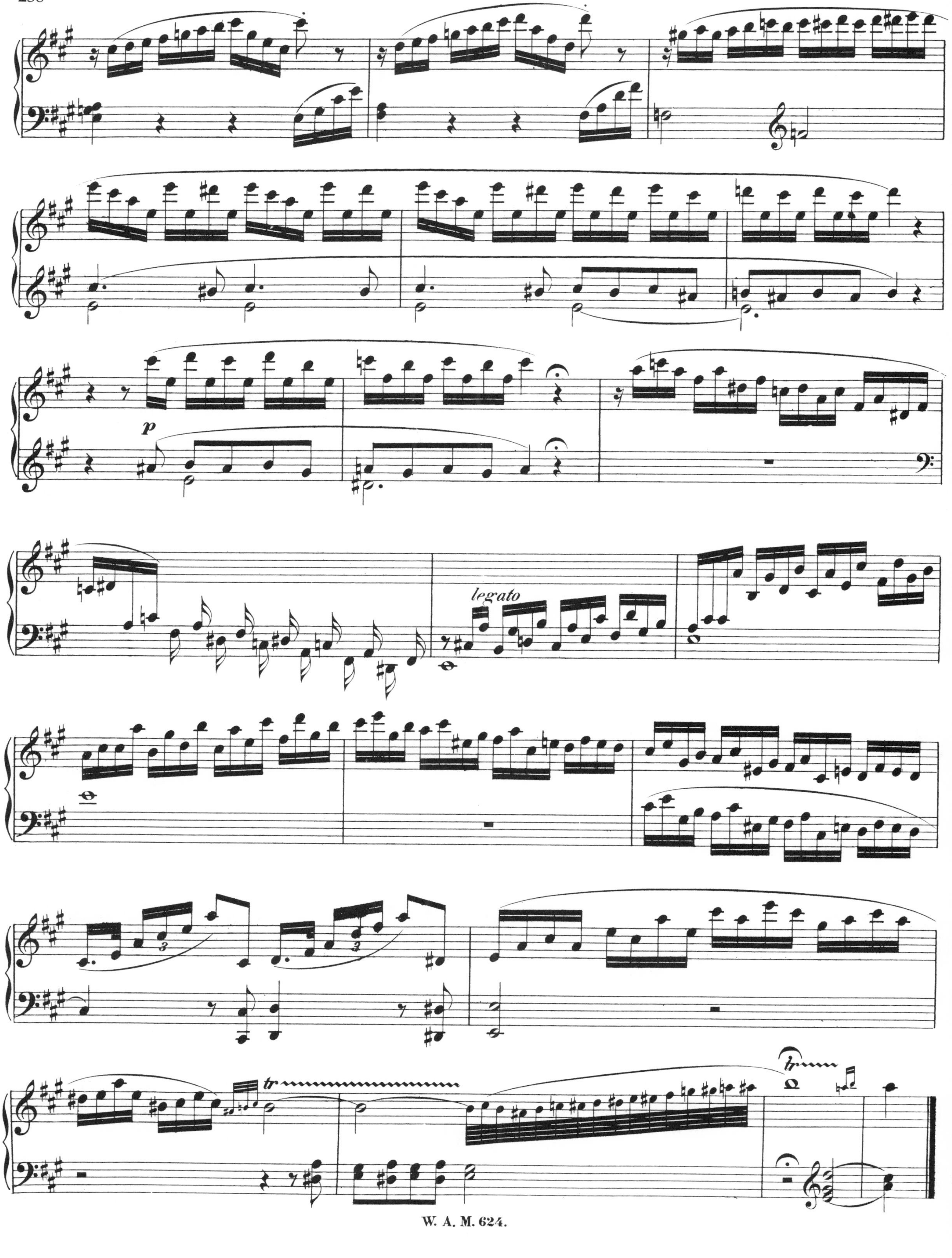
p
legato
tr

Concerto No. 12, 1st Movement

Concerto No. 12, 2nd Movement

Concerto No. 12, 2nd Movement

Cadenza per l' Andante.

Concerto No. 12, 2nd Movement, after first fermata

Concerto No. 12, 3rd Movement

Concerto No. 12, 3rd Movement

Concerto No. 12, 3rd Movement, after last fermata

Adagio.

Concerto No. 13, 1st Movement

Concerto No. 13, 2nd Movement

Concerto No. 13, 3rd Movement (measure 120)

Concerto No. 14, 1st Movement

W. A. M. 624.

Concerto No. 15, 1st Movement

Concerto No. 15, 3rd Movement

Concerto No. 15, 3rd Movement, after first fermata

Concerto No. 16, 1st Movement

Concerto No. 16, 3rd Movement